FEROCIOUS FIGHTING ANIMALS

DINGOES

Julia J. Quinlan

PowerKiDS
press.

New York

Published in 2013 by The Rosen Publishing Group, Inc.
29 East 21st Street, New York, NY 10010

First Edition

Editor: Amelie von Zumbusch
Book Design: Andrew Povolny

Photo Credits: Cover Paul Nevin/Photolibrary/Getty Images; pp. 4, 10–11, 21 Martin Harvey/Peter Arnold/Getty Images; pp. 5, 8, 16 (left),16 (right) iStockphoto/Thinkstock; pp. 6, 9 Jason Edwards/National Geographic Image Collection/Getty Images; p. 7 Julie Fletcher/Flickr/Getty Images; ;pp. 12–13, 14, 17 © Ardea/Ferrero, John Paul/AnimalsAnimals; p. 15 Hemera/Thinkstock; p. 18 © iStockphoto.com/Craig Dingle; p. 19 Ronald Sumners/Shutterstock.com; p. 20 Houshmand Rabbani/Shutterstock.com; p. 22 SF photo/Shutterstock.com.

Library of Congress Cataloging-in-Publication Data

Quinlan, Julia J.
 Dingoes / by Julia J. Quinlan. — 1st ed.
     p. cm. — (Ferocious fighting animals)
 Includes index.
 ISBN 978-1-4488-9675-2 (library binding) — ISBN 978-1-4488-9808-4 (pbk.) —
 ISBN 978-1-4488-9809-1 (6-pack)
 1. Dingo—Juvenile literature. I. Title.
 QL737.C22Q46 2013
 599.77'2—dc23
                                      2012029107

Manufactured in the United States of America

CPSIA Compliance Information: Batch #W13PK5: For Further Information contact Rosen Publishing, New York, New York at 1-800-237-9932

CONTENTS

WILD DOGS!

At first glance, dingoes might look like regular dogs. However, they are quite different. Dingoes are wild dogs that have **evolved** to be fierce hunters and fighters. They can survive in the harshest **habitats**. They are ferocious **predators** that hunt animals of any size. They use their speed, strong jaws, and sharp teeth to catch and kill their **prey**.

It is against the law to keep dingoes as pets in some parts of Australia.

Dingoes are related to the dogs that people keep as pets. Some people do keep dingoes as pets, but they need a lot of training in order to be safe around humans. Dingoes are best suited to the wild parts of Australia.

The warrigal is another name for the dingo.

WHERE DO DINGOES LIVE?

Dingoes are most famous for living in Australia. However, they also live in parts of Southeast Asia. There are dingoes in Thailand and Malaysia. The dingoes that live in Australia are **descended** from Asian dingoes that were brought over by seafarers. Dingoes first came to Australia over 3,500 years ago.

Dingoes are found in most of the parts of the Australian Outback. The Outback is the dry, inland part of Australia where few people live.

These dingoes are in the Painted Desert, in South Australia.

Dingoes live in every Australian state except Tasmania, which is an island off Australia's southeast coast. They can live in almost any habitat. They can be found in hot deserts, wet rain forests, and on snowy mountains. Dingoes are tough enough to live anywhere!

FURRY AND FEROCIOUS

Dingoes look similar to regular dogs. They can be up to 2 feet (60 cm) tall and 4 feet (1 m) long. Dingoes have bushy tails that are about 12 inches (30 cm) long. Dingoes weigh between 22 and 30 pounds (10–14 kg).

Dingoes with yellow and reddish fur are common in sandy areas. Dingoes with black or dark tan fur are more often found in forests.

Most dingoes have golden or reddish fur. Some have black or brown fur. Dingoes usually have lighter fur on their bellies. They have big, perky ears and dark, almond-shaped eyes. Dingoes look like the kind of dog you might want to go up to and pet, but don't let their cute appearance fool you!

Male dingoes are larger than female dingoes.

HOWLING PACKS

Dingoes often live together in groups called packs. A pack can have up to 10 dingoes. One male and one female dingo lead each pack. These two are the **dominant** dingoes in the pack. Packs have **territories** where they live and hunt. The size of their territory depends on where they live and how easy it is to find food.

Dingoes **communicate** with each other through howls. Dingoes howl to find other dingoes and to scare away dingoes that are not pack members. Dingo packs often howl together. Dingoes do not bark often, as **domesticated** dogs do. Dingoes also communicate through scent marking.

Dingoes spend some time alone but also meet up regularly with the other members of their pack.

FEROCIOUS DINGOES

Dingoes will fight large prey, such as the lace monitor here. Dingoes also fight with dingoes from other packs. You wouldn't want to fight a dingo! Dingoes can be dangerous to humans. They have been known to attack people and even kill children.

DINGO PUPS

Dingo babies are called pups. Female dingoes give birth to a litter of around five pups. Dingoes have babies once a year. Female dingoes give birth in dens. The pups drink their mothers' milk. Pups are raised by the pack. All of the dingoes in a pack will help keep the dominant pair's pups safe.

This dingo is curled up with its pups in its den. Dingoes use caves as dens. They also use dens dug by other animals and make dens under hollow logs.

Dingo pups stay with their mothers until they are six to eight months old.

Dingo moms can be vicious. The dominant female in a pack will often kill the pups of other females in the pack. Dingoes can live up to six years in the wild. Dingoes that are cared for by humans can live for 15 years.

DINGO PREY

Dingoes eat a wide range of prey. They hunt small animals such as geese, rabbits, and lizards. They also go after larger prey such as kangaroos and wallabies. Dingoes hunt mostly at night. They hunt smaller animals alone. When hunting larger prey, dingoes hunt in packs.

The red kangaroo (left) and swamp wallaby (right) are two animals that dingoes commonly hunt.

Dingoes use their powerful jaws and teeth to bite the necks of their prey.

Dingoes are often blamed for attacks on farm animals. However, the attackers are more often **feral** dogs, or domestic dogs that live in the wild. Dingoes in Asia live much closer to humans than Australian dingoes. Asian dingoes eat trash left by humans and food that humans give them.

AN APEX PREDATOR

Dingoes are **apex predators** in Australia. That means they do not have any natural predators. They are the largest warm-blooded predator in Australia. Dingoes do have some enemies, though. Crocodiles sometimes kill them. Dingoes are also killed by other dingoes or by feral dogs. When they need to, dingoes defend themselves by fighting and biting.

Dingoes will come into areas where people live if they cannot find food elsewhere.

The system of fences that keeps dingoes away from sheep and other farm animals was built in the 1880s.

Humans are responsible for many dingo deaths. Many people view dingoes as pests because they have a reputation for killing farm animals. There have been several long fences put up in Australia to try and keep dingoes away from people and farm animals.

HELPFUL DINGOES

Dingoes play an important role in the **ecosystem**. They keep unwanted animal **populations** under control. For example, dingoes love to eat rabbits. Rabbits are an **invasive species** in Australia. They are not native to Australia and can damage the ecosystem. Dingoes help control the rabbit population.

Rabbits are a big problem in Australia. They cause millions of dollars of damage to crops each year.

Predators, such as dingoes, are an important part of any ecosystem.

Dingoes also hunt feral animals such as cats, dogs, and goats. These feral animals are also invasive species. When they live in the wild, they compete with native Australian species for food. This leaves native Australian animals with less food. Thanks to invasive species, some Australian animals are at risk of dying out.

DINGOES AT RISK

The future of dingoes is uncertain. The population of pure dingoes is going down. This is mostly because dingoes mate with domestic and feral dogs. The more dingoes mate with other species, the fewer dingoes there will be. Some people also keep dingoes as pets and try to make them domesticated.

Wild dingoes are an important part of Australia's ecosystem. Though they can be dangerous, it is important that they be protected. Luckily, there are many groups working to save the dingo.

Some dingoes live in national parks, where they are protected. This dingo is in Great Sandy National Park, in Queensland, Australia.

GLOSSARY

apex predators (AY-peks PREH-duh-terz) Predators that are at the top of their food chains.

communicate (kuh-MYOO-nih-kayt) To share facts or feelings.

descended (dih-SEN-did) Born of a certain family or group.

domesticated (duh-MES-tih-kayt-ed) Raised to live with people.

dominant (DAH-mih-nent) In charge.

ecosystem (EE-koh-sis-tem) A community of living things and the surroundings in which they live.

evolved (ih-VOLVD) Changed over many years.

feral (FER-al) An animal that used to live with people but that has gone back to the wild.

habitats (HA-buh-tats) The kinds of land where animals or plants naturally live.

invasive species (in-VAY-siv SPEE-sheez) Plants or animals that are brought to a place and drive out the plants and animals that naturally live there.

populations (pop-yoo-LAY-shunz) Groups of animals or people living in the same place.

predators (PREH-duh-terz) Animals that kill other animals for food.

prey (PRAY) An animal that is hunted by another animal for food.

territories (TER-uh-tor-eez) Land or spaces that animals guard for their use.

INDEX

WEBSITES

Due to the changing nature of Internet links, PowerKids Press has developed an online list of websites related to the subject of this book. This site is updated regularly. Please use this link to access the list: www.powerkidslinks.com/ffa/dingo/